AF269976

King Penguin

by Julie Murray

Abdo Kids Jumbo is an Imprint of Abdo Kids
abdobooks.com

abdobooks.com

Published by Abdo Kids, a division of ABDO, P.O. Box 398166, Minneapolis, Minnesota 55439.
Copyright © 2025 by Abdo Consulting Group, Inc. International copyrights reserved in all countries.
No part of this book may be reproduced in any form without written permission from the publisher.
Abdo Kids Jumbo™ is a trademark and logo of Abdo Kids.

Printed in the United States of America, North Mankato, Minnesota.

102024

012025

THIS BOOK CONTAINS
RECYCLED MATERIALS

Photo Credits: Getty Images, Shutterstock

Production Contributors: Teddy Borth, Jennie Forsberg, Grace Hansen
Design Contributors: Candice Keimig, Pakou Moua

Library of Congress Control Number: 2024936621
Publisher's Cataloging-in-Publication Data

Names: Murray, Julie, author.

Title: King penguin / by Julie Murray

Description: Minneapolis, Minnesota : Abdo Kids, 2025 | Series: Royal animals | Includes online resources
    and index.

Identifiers: ISBN 9798384902980 (lib. bdg.) | ISBN 9798384903680 (ebook) | ISBN 9798384904038
    (Read-to-me ebook)

Subjects: LCSH: King penguin--Juvenile literature. | Penguins--Juvenile literature. | Birds--Juvenile
    literature. | Subantarctic Islands (N.Z.)--Juvenile literature. | Animal kingdom--Juvenile literature.

Classification: DDC 598.47--dc23

Table of Contents

The King Penguin

The king penguin is the second-largest penguin in the world. It is mainly found on the islands surrounding Antarctica. It lives near the sea in valleys and on shores.

Africa
South America
Antarctica
King Penguin Range
Australia

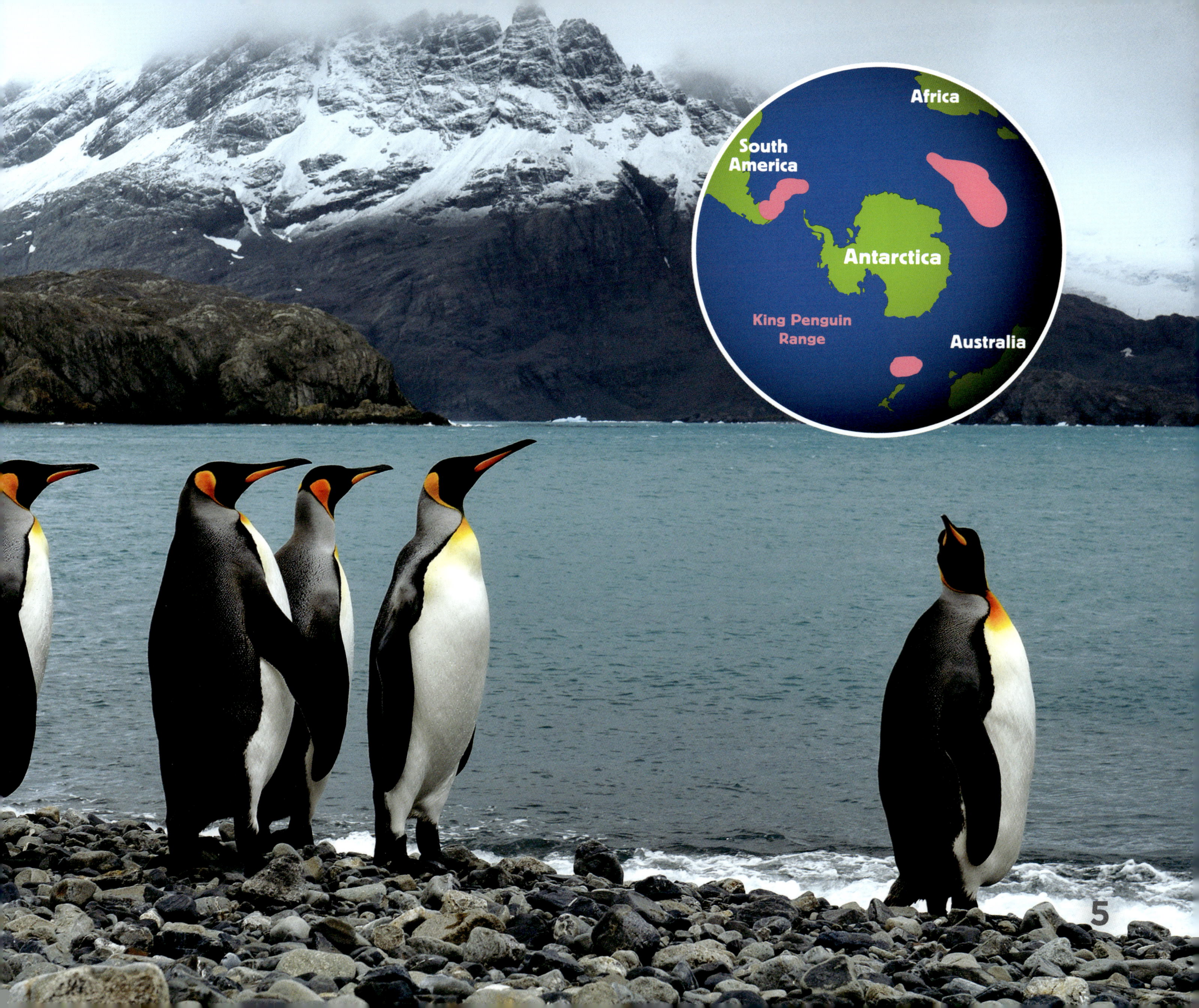

5

The king penguin got its royal name because it was once thought to be the largest penguin **species**. However, the emperor penguin is larger.

king
penguin
emperor
penguin

Body

King penguins stand about 30 to 37 inches (76-94 cm) tall. They often weigh between 30 and 40 pounds (14-18 kg).

Their bellies are white. Their
heads and backs are covered
in black and silvery-gray
feathers. They have orange
markings on their upper
chests, heads, and beaks.

Molting

King penguins **molt** every year. This change takes four weeks to complete. They do not eat during this time. They lose more than 40% of their body fat!

Food

King penguins hunt for food in the water. Fish make up 80% of their diet. King penguins also eat **krill** and squid.

Baby King Penguins

King penguins form huge groups called **colonies** to live together and **breed**. Some colonies have more than 200,000 penguins!

Females lay one egg each year. Both parents take turns keeping the egg warm and safe. They put it on top of their feet and cover it with their body. The egg hatches in about 55 days.

As the chick grows, it joins its

own group called a crèche.

Chicks are fully grown after

about 15 months.

More Facts

- A king penguin can dive more than 300 feet (91 m) deep. It can stay under water for up to 10 minutes.

- A king penguin's favorite food is a tiny fish called a lantern fish. A king penguin can eat up to 2,000 fish in a day!

- King penguins feed their chicks by **regurgitating** food into their mouths.

Glossary

breed – to produce offspring.

colony – a group of animals of the same type living closely together.

krill – tiny shrimp-like crustaceans that feed on plankton.

molt – to shed or cast off feathers and grow a new covering.

regurgitating – bringing swallowed food back up again to the mouth.

species – animals that look alike and can have young together.

Index